Francis Frith's
NEW FOREST

◆

PHOTOGRAPHIC MEMORIES

Francis Frith's
NEW FOREST

◆

John Bainbridge

FRITH BOOK Co

First published in the United Kingdom in 2000 by
Frith Book Company Ltd

British Library Cataloguing in Publication Data

New Forest
John Bainbridge
ISBN 1-85937-128-0

Frith Book Company Ltd
Frith's Barn, Teffont,
Salisbury, Wiltshire SP3 5QP
Tel: +44 (0) 1722 716 376
Email: info@frithbook.co.uk
www.frithbook.co.uk

Printed and bound in Great Britain

Front Cover: Ringwood, The Millstream 1900 45027

CONTENTS

FRANCIS FRITH: *Victorian Pioneer*

FRANCIS FRITH, Victorian founder of the world-famous photographic archive, was a complex and multitudinous man. A devout Quaker and a highly successful Victorian businessman, he was both philosophic by nature and pioneering in outlook.

By 1855 Francis Frith had already established a wholesale grocery business in Liverpool, and sold it for the astonishing sum of £200,000, which is the equivalent today of over £15,000,000. Now a multi-millionaire, he was able to indulge his passion for travel. As a child he had pored over travel books written by early explorers, and his fancy and imagination had been stirred by family holidays to the sublime mountain regions of Wales and Scotland. 'What a land of spirit-stirring and enriching scenes and places!' he had written. He was to return to these scenes of grandeur in later years to 'recapture the thousands of vivid and tender memories', but with a different purpose. Now in his thirties, and captivated by the new science of photography, Frith

set out on a series of pioneering journeys to the Nile regions that occupied him from 1856 until 1860.

INTRIGUE AND ADVENTURE

He took with him on his travels a specially-designed wicker carriage that acted as both dark-room and sleeping chamber. These far-flung journeys were packed with intrigue and adventure. In his life story, written when he was sixty-three, Frith tells of being held captive by bandits, and of fighting 'an awful midnight battle to the very point of surrender with a deadly pack of hungry, wild dogs'. Sporting flowing Arab costume, Frith arrived at Akaba by camel seventy years before Lawrence, where he encountered 'desert princes and rival sheikhs, blazing with jewel-hilted swords'.

During these extraordinary adventures he was assiduously exploring the desert regions bordering the Nile and patiently recording the antiquities and peoples with his camera. He was the first photographer to venture beyond the sixth cataract. Africa was still the mysterious 'Dark Continent', and Stanley and Livingstone's historic meeting was a decade into the future. The conditions for picture taking confound belief. He laboured for hours in his wicker dark-room in the sweltering heat of the desert, while the volatile chemicals fizzed dangerously in their trays. Often he was forced to work in remote tombs and caves where conditions were cooler. Back in London he exhibited his photographs and was 'rapturously cheered' by members of the Royal Society. His reputation as a photographer was made overnight. An eminent modern historian has likened their impact on the population of the time to that on our own generation of the first photographs taken on the surface of the moon.

VENTURE OF A LIFE-TIME

Characteristically, Frith quickly spotted the opportunity to create a new business as a specialist publisher of photographs. He lived in an era of immense and sometimes violent change. For the poor in the early part of Victoria's reign work was a drudge and the hours long, and people had precious little free time to enjoy themselves.

Most had no transport other than a cart or gig at their disposal, and had not travelled far beyond the boundaries of their own town or village. However, by the 1870s, the railways had threaded their way across the country, and Bank Holidays and half-day Saturdays had been made obligatory by Act of Parliament. All of a sudden the ordinary working man and his family were able to enjoy days out and see a little more of the world.

With characteristic business acumen, Francis Frith foresaw that these new tourists would enjoy having souvenirs to commemorate their days out. In 1860 he married Mary Ann Rosling and set out with the intention of photographing every city, town and village in Britain. For the next thirty years he travelled the country by train and by pony and trap, producing fine photographs of seaside resorts and beauty spots that were keenly bought by millions of Victorians. These prints were painstakingly pasted into family albums and pored over during the dark nights of winter, rekindling precious memories of summer excursions.

THE RISE OF FRITH & CO

Frith's studio was soon supplying retail shops all over the country. To meet the demand he gathered about him a small team of photographers, and published the work of independent artist-photographers of the calibre of Roger Fenton and Francis Bedford. In order to gain some understanding of the scale of Frith's business one only has to look at the catalogue issued by Frith & Co in 1886: it runs to some 670

pages, listing not only many thousands of views of the British Isles but also many photographs of most European countries, and China, Japan, the USA and Canada – note the sample page shown above from the hand-written *Frith & Co* ledgers detailing pictures taken. By 1890 Frith had created the greatest specialist photographic publishing company in the world, with over 2,000 outlets – more than the combined number that Boots and WH Smith have today! The picture on the right shows the *Frith & Co* display board at Ingleton in the Yorkshire Dales. Beautifully constructed with mahogany frame and gilt inserts, it could display up to a dozen local scenes.

POSTCARD BONANZA

◆

The ever-popular holiday postcard we know today took many years to develop. In 1870 the Post Office issued the first plain cards, with a pre-printed stamp on one face. In 1894 they allowed other publishers' cards to be sent through the mail with an attached adhesive halfpenny stamp. Demand grew rapidly, and in 1895 a new size of postcard was permitted called the

court card, but there was little room for illustration. In 1899, a year after Frith's death, a new card measuring 5.5 x 3.5 inches became the standard format, but it was not until 1902 that the divided back came into being, with address and message on one face and a full-size illustration on the other. *Frith & Co* were in the vanguard of postcard development, and Frith's sons Eustace and Cyril continued their father's monumental task, expanding the number of views offered to the public and recording more and more places in Britain, as the coasts and countryside were opened up to mass travel.

Francis Frith died in 1898 at his villa in Cannes, his great project still growing. The archive he created continued in business for another seventy years. By 1970 it contained over a third of a million pictures of 7,000 cities, towns and villages. The massive photographic record Frith has left to us stands as a living monument to a special and very remarkable man.

Frith's Archive: *A Unique Legacy*

FRANCIS FRITH'S legacy to us today is of immense significance and value, for the magnificent archive of evocative photographs he created provides a unique record of change in 7,000 cities, towns and villages throughout Britain over a century and more. Frith and his fellow studio photographers revisited locations many times down the years to update their views, compiling for us an enthralling and colourful pageant of British life and character.

We tend to think of Frith's sepia views of Britain as nostalgic, for most of us use them to conjure up memories of places in our own lives with which we have family associations. It often makes us forget that to Francis Frith they were records of daily life as it was actually being lived in the cities, towns and villages of his day. The Victorian

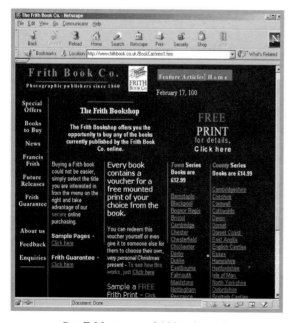

See Frith at www. frithbook.co.uk

age was one of great and often bewildering change for ordinary people, and though the pictures evoke an impression of slower times, life was as busy and hectic as it is today.

We are fortunate that Frith was a photographer of the people, dedicated to recording the minutiae of everyday life. For it is this sheer wealth of visual data, the painstaking chronicle of changes in dress, transport, street layouts, buildings, housing, engineering and landscape that captivates us so much today. His remarkable images offer us a powerful link with the past and with the lives of our ancestors.

TODAY'S TECHNOLOGY

Computers have now made it possible for Frith's many thousands of images to be accessed almost instantly. In the Frith archive today, each photograph is carefully 'digitised' then stored on a CD Rom. Frith archivists can locate a single photograph amongst thousands within seconds. Views can be catalogued and sorted under a variety of categories of place and content to the immediate benefit of researchers. Inexpensive reference prints can be created for them at the touch of a mouse button, and a wide range of books and other printed materials assembled and published for a wider, more general readership - in the next twelve months over a hundred Frith local history titles will be published! The day-to-day workings of the archive are very different from how they were in Francis Frith's time: imagine the herculean task of sorting through eleven tons of glass negatives as Frith had to do to locate a particular sequence of pictures! Yet the archive still prides itself on maintaining the same high standards of excellence laid down by Francis Frith, including the painstaking cataloguing and indexing of every view.

It is curious to reflect on how the internet now allows researchers in America and elsewhere greater instant access to the archive than Frith himself ever enjoyed. Many thousands of individual views can be called up on screen within seconds on one of the Frith internet sites, enabling people living continents away to revisit the streets of their ancestral home town, or view places in Britain where they have enjoyed holidays. Many overseas researchers welcome the chance to view special theme selections, such as transport, sports, costume and ancient monuments.

We are certain that Francis Frith would have heartily approved of these modern developments, for he himself was always working at the very limits of Victorian photographic technology.

THE VALUE OF THE ARCHIVE TODAY

Because of the benefits brought by the computer, Frith's images are increasingly studied by social historians, by researchers into genealogy and ancestory, by architects, town planners, and by teachers and schoolchildren involved in local history projects. In addition, the archive offers every one of us a unique opportunity to examine the places where we and our families have lived and worked down the years. Immensely successful in Frith's own era, the archive is now, a century and more on, entering a new phase of popularity.

THE PAST IN TUNE WITH THE FUTURE

Historians consider the Francis Frith Collection to be of prime national importance. It is the only archive of its kind remaining in private ownership and has been valued at a million pounds. However, this figure is now rapidly increasing as digital technology enables more and more people around the world to enjoy its benefits.

Francis Frith's archive is now housed in an historic timber barn in the beautiful village of Teffont in Wiltshire. Its founder would not recognize the archive office as it is today. In place of the many thousands of dusty boxes containing glass plate negatives and an all-pervading odour of photographic chemicals, there are now ranks of computer screens. He would be amazed to watch his images travelling round the world at unimaginable speeds through network and internet lines.

The archive's future is both bright and exciting. Francis Frith, with his unshakeable belief in making photographs available to the greatest number of people, would undoubtedly approve of what is being done today with his lifetime's work. His photographs, depicting our shared past, are now bringing pleasure and enlightenment to millions around the world a century and more after his death.

IN THE HEART OF THE FOREST

SOME PEOPLE VISITING the New Forest for the first time assume that they will find a great expanse of trees; they are often surprised at the open nature of much of the countryside - the great stretches of wild heathland and the lawns, close-cropped by ponies and deer. Though there are woodlands a-plenty, the word 'forest' in this sense means an area of wilderness, particularly one held by the Crown for hunting.

William the Conqueror took control of this region and created his 'New' Forest in 1079. A later chronicler recorded that 'the Conqueror took away much land from God and men, and converted it to the use of wild beasts and the sport of his dogs'. The boundaries of the original Forest were much more extensive than those we know today, taking in much of the land between the River Avon and Southampton Water, right down to the southern coastline. The creation of the royal hunting forest was clearly a considerable intrusion into the lives of local people, though the allegation made by early commentators that William 'destroyed thirty-six churches and exterminated their inhabitants' cannot be sustained.

The hunting forests of the Norman period had their own set of laws, as though they were separate kingdoms within the realm of England. It became an offence to hunt, wound or kill the king's deer, to strike a forest officer, or to cut vert in what had previously been open countryside. Punishments could be severe, ranging from long periods of imprisonment to mutilation or death. Life went on in the surrounding communities in the best way possible given these restrictions.

Later monarchs relaxed the rules somewhat, though interestingly Charles I - in one of those fits of absolutism that were to eventually cost him his head - tried to bring them back with much of the harshness of his Norman ancestors. Commissions in Queen Victoria's time led to legislation in 1851 which removed the right of the Crown to harbour deer in the New Forest, giving the landscape back to the people. The same Act led to the unfortunate enclosure of some of the Forest's open spaces, though, nevertheless, there has always been a strong tradition of free access for walkers and riders.

One historical event in the long history of the New Forest overshadows all others. On 2nd August 1100 the Conqueror's son King

William II, nicknamed Rufus, set off into the Forest on a hunting expedition with his brother Henry and a number of nobles including Sir Walter Tyrrell. At some point during the chase, or so tradition alleges, Tyrrell fired an arrow which killed the King. Some later chroniclers, and the inscription on the Rufus Stone which now marks the locality of the deed, imply that this was a pure accident, Tyrrell's arrow glancing off a tree or the back of a hunted beast before striking down William Rufus. But it is more than likely that this was the carefully planned political assassination of an unpopular ruler. After the death, William Rufus' brother Henry rode at full gallop to Winchester to seize the royal treasure and to seek the support of the Church for his claim to the succession. Tyrrell fled to Normandy and spent the rest of his life - even on his death bed - denying that he had fired the fatal shot. His claims of innocence might well be justified, for William Rufus had many enemies, not least his brother Henry who succeeded him to the throne. William Rufus was buried without ceremony in Winchester Cathedral.

Walking through the lonelier spots of the New Forest it is not difficult to get a feeling of what the old hunting forest must have been like. Some of the old Forest Laws and traditions remain, curious echoes of our feudal past. The inhabitants of many of the oldest cottages still hold Common Rights to graze livestock, and Agisters are still appointed to collect payment on the headage out in the Forest. Colt-hunting, the regular round-up of the ponies, still survives, all noise and spectacle, while the Verderers Court continues to meet five times a year at Lyndhurst to sort out Forest disputes.

In 1999 the Government announced that it intended that the New Forest should become a National Park, so that this unique and outstandingly beautiful landscape could receive greater protection as we enter the 21st century. A thousand years ago an absolute king used legislation to seize the New Forest for his own pleasures. A millennium later it is perhaps fitting that new legislation should confirm that the New Forest must be preserved as the common heritage of all.

NEW FOREST PONIES c1955 N18001

BOLDREWOOD, KING AND QUEEN OAKS 1890 25586

Here we see a New Forest glade under the shade of the famous King and Queen Oaks. It is said that although other English forests have taller oak trees, none have so shapely a collection of old oaks as the New Forest.

THE KNIGHTWOOD OAK 1890 25587

The celebrated Knightwood Oak is pictured here at a time when its girth was already over 17 feet. It is the profusion of trees that makes the New Forest a splendid place to visit, particularly in the spring when the leaves are fresh and green, or in the autumn when the trees present foliage of the richest browns and golds.

THE RUFUS STONE 1890 25585

THE RUFUS STONE 1890
The stone reads: 'Here stood the oak tree on which an arrow shot by Sir Walter Tyrrell at a stag glanced and struck King William the Second surnamed Rufus on the breast of which he instantly died on the second day of August Anno 1100'.

◆

THE RUFUS STONE c1955
William Rufus' brother Richard also met his death in the New Forest by 'a pestilential blast', while the King's nephew - also called Richard - died either by being shot by an arrow or by strangulation after being caught up in the boughs of a tree - an uncanny trio of coincidences.

THE RUFUS STONE c1955 N18017

OLD ROMAN BRIDGE 1908 60124

QUEEN'S BOWER 1908 60125

OLD ROMAN BRIDGE 1908
A Roman road ran this way. The Romans took a great interest in the New Forest. It supplied wood and charcoal to fire kilns for the manufacture of pottery or for the smelting of iron.

◆

QUEEN'S BOWER 1908
Nobody knows for sure why this delightful corner of the Forest is called Queen's Bower. The origins of the name are lost in the mists of antiquity. The little wooden bridge and the three flowing streams that meet here make this a favourite walking destination.

NEW FOREST PONIES 1913 65636A
The famous New Forest ponies are only wild in the sense that they are not broken in. All of the ponies are owned by someone, though they may stay out in the Forest through all the seasons of the year.

ON THE BROCKENHURST ROAD 1918 68041
Some people are fortunate enough to live away from the towns and in the heart of the New Forest, their old cottages looking as much a part of nature as the trees and furze. It is difficult to estimate how many Forest dwellers lost their homes with the creation of William's hunting forest.

NEW FOREST PONIES c1955 N18001

An old New Forest tradition alleges that the ponies are the descendants of Spanish horses that swam ashore from the wrecked galleons of the Spanish Armada. Sad to relate, there appears to be no truth in this interesting old legend.

PIGS NEAR BROOK c1955 N18004

Many original farms in the New Forest had the ancient common right of pannage, the right to turn out pigs into the Forest to feed on mast and acorns. In 1848 a commission allowed this old right to continue between September 25th and November 22nd - the so-called 'Pannage Month'.

NEW FOREST PONIES, SWAN GREEN C1955 N18014

Many of the cottages inside the Forest boundary are of considerable antiquity, being either renovations or replacements of buildings that have stood on the same sites for centuries; it is hard to imagine today just what an isolated existence would have been the lot of New Forest inhabitants even a hundred years ago.

NEW FOREST PONIES c1955 N18025

Superstitions lingered in the New Forest longer than in many places and are still recounted. Ill-fortune is still occasionally blamed upon a mischievous elf called Laurence. The old saying 'He's got a touch of Laurence' implies lazy behaviour.

NEW FOREST PONIES c1965 N18047

The true New Forest pony can survive outdoors through all seasons, eating holly and furze tops during the winter. Ponies were used as pack animals in and around the Forest - not least by smugglers.

NEW FOREST PONIES c1955 N18069

In size the New Forest ponies range from eleven to thirteen hands, and their wild life-style keeps them rangy and fit. Much good work has been done by the New Forest breeding project to keep the breed pure.

LYNDHURST, CHARCOAL BURNING IN THE FOREST c1955 L123013

Charcoal burning was one of the New Forest's earliest industries, though it is a rarer occurrence today. The charcoal produced had a multitude of uses, particularly in the smelting of iron. Elizabeth I became so concerned at the loss of trees, at a time when England needed timber for ships, that she passed a law preventing the felling of trees for charcoal production.

VILLAGES OF THE NEW FOREST

THE VILLAGES IN and around the New Forest are mostly of considerable antiquity, each having their place in the longer history of England. To delve into the past of any of them would be a worthwhile project for anyone with more than a passing interest in earlier times. Most of these villages have been shaped by the presence nearby of the New Forest itself.

Tradition alleges that William the Conqueror swept away a large number of villages in his desire to dedicate the New Forest to his favourite pursuit - hunting. But there is only a touch of truth in the legend. Much of the land would have been unproductive in agricultural terms, and contained only the villages it could have supported. William himself would have wanted only wilder countryside for the chase, and there were probably few people actually living in the areas taken in.

This is not to suggest that the neighbouring villages we know of today did not suffer for the sake of William's pleasures. Domesday Book gives examples of villages that lost woodland and heath to the 'New' Forest. Some - not all - received a rent reduction for lost land. But any removal of taxation has to be matched against the inability of local people to hunt for game for the table, to cut vert and to graze livestock quite as freely as they once did. Villagers would have had to contend with harsh Forest Laws as part of their daily life.

Despite all of these problems, many of the New Forest's villages survived and prospered despite the nearby hunting forest. Some were useful for agricultural production, or as the setting for corn-grinding mills. In the course of time a number fell under the control of other nobility than the monarch, or under the protection of the Church - a potent power that even medieval kings did little to offend if they were wise.

Perhaps the best time to visit the villages of the New Forest is in the early morning, or in the evening, when the cars and coaches are fewer and there are fewer people about. This will give a better idea of just how isolated these communities were until well into the 20th century. The Forest which swept in around them, its trees overshadowing church and cottages, was even wilder then; the deer were often to be found in the village streets.

In those earlier days the villages made few concessions to tourism. Well into Victoria's reign, any passing travellers would have had to content themselves with rough and ready village inns or a hard bed in a local cottage if they wanted to stay the night in the wild and lonely interior of the New Forest. Victoria herself finally severed the links between royalty and the old hunting forest, decreeing that it should be given over for the populace to enjoy. Although the New Forest had been visited, studied and written about before then, notably by the 18th-century parson-naturalist William Gilpin in his delightful and still relevant 'Remarks on Forest Scenery, illustrated by the New Forest', tourism as we know it dates to Queen Victoria's kind gesture.

Today most visitors come to the New Forest for the day from the neighbouring towns and cities, or from the seaside resorts such as Bournemouth and Christchurch. In a way, that is a pity. Actually staying in a New Forest village is a great way to absorb the atmosphere of the living community and the lovely wilderness beyond. Villagers know a great deal about the surrounding countryside and their own communities in particular - perhaps the very best way to discover the many delights of the New Forest.

EMERY DOWN, THE NEW FOREST INN c1960 E196019

ALDERHOLT, THE MEMORIAL AND THE CHURCH c1960 A310002
On the border between Dorset and Hampshire, Alderholt lies on the edge of the great medieval hunting ground of Cranborne Chase. In early hunting parlance a forest was a hunting ground in the exclusive possession of the monarch; a chase was the preserve of minor royalty, the nobility or a gentleman.

ALDERHOLT, THE MILL c1960 A310008
There has been a mill at Alderholt for generations; as with so many mills in southern England, this one was used for its original purpose until recently - in historic terms. Here some youngsters enjoy a spot of angling in the mill stream.

ALDERHOLT, THE CHURCHILL ARMS c1960 A310016

Alderholt was an ancient settlement even before the Saxons came to live here and gave the village a name. On the downlands close by are a considerable number of prehistoric barrows - burial grounds of some of the earliest inhabitants.

ALDERHOLT, THE OLD CHAPEL c1960 A310003

An older chapel at Alderholt fell into ruin during the reign of Charles II. The original was used by huntsmen to bless their expeditions into the wilderness of Cranborne Chase. The replacement gives an idea of how the earlier chapel might have looked.

ALDERHOLT, THE SCHOOL c1960 A310001

ALDERHOLT
The School **c1960**
The village school is an integral part of a rural community, allowing children to be educated close to home. Older youngsters often have to go further afield to complete their education.

◆

ALDERHOLT
Fordingbridge Road **c1960**
Once surrounded by the deer-haunted woods and heaths of Cranborne Chase, Alderholt has kept much of its original character, despite some new houses and a church of little antiquity; the latter is a building of charm, for all its newness.

ALDERHOLT, FORDINGBRIDGE ROAD c1960 A310020

BEAULIEU, THE ABBEY 1908 60484

Beaulieu village lies not far from Lymington, at the head of the Beaulieu River, and is attractive in itself. But most visitors come to see the old Abbey, founded by King John in 1204 and ransacked by Henry VIII in 1539.

BEAULIEU, THE ABBEY CHURCH 1908 60477

Many of the Abbey ruins remain, and some of the buildings are still in use. Close by the altar of the Abbey church lies the body of Isabella, wife of Richard, Earl of Cornwall, the second son of the founder King John. Other historical figures sought sanctuary at the Abbey, including Margaret of Anjou, Lady Warwick and the rebellious Perkin Warbeck.

BEAULIEU, THE LAKE 1908 60475
Beaulieu is now the home of the Montagu family. Close to the Abbey is the National Motor Museum, a splendid collection of cars founded by Lord Montagu of Beaulieu.

BOLDRE, THE CHURCH c1960 B694001
Boldre (pronounced Bolder) church stands apart from its village and dates back to the time of the Norman kings. The Poet Laureate Robert Southey married Caroline Bowles here, while the naturalist William Gilpin lies buried in the churchyard. There is a fine memorial to the crew of HMS Hood - sunk by the German pocket battleship Bismarck in 1941.

BRANSGORE, THE VILLAGE c1960 B695007

Bransgore, a few miles from Bournemouth, is a beautiful village of considerable antiquity, just outside the present boundary of the New Forest. It stood here for centuries before the neighbouring resort had a single house. Despite some modern building, it remains as attractive as this photograph suggests.

BRANSGORE, THE CHURCH c1960 B695004

Bransgore's present church is a mostly Victorian structure, though its exquisitely carved font, transported here from Christchurch Priory, is 16th-century. The old Litany Desk commemorates parishioner Henry Nicholson, 'a chief musician in this House of God'.

BRANSGORE, THE POST OFFICE c1960 B695001

BRANSGORE
The Post Office **c1960**
Village shops continued to prosper until the late 20th century, when trips to neighbouring supermarkets became the fashion. Dallard's corner shop, seen here before the shopping exodus, has a wide variety of goods on sale.

◆

BRANSGORE
The Crown Inn **c1960**
Village public houses are still the heart of many communities around the New Forest - not only as places to go for refreshments, but as places to meet and socialise, and as venues for sports clubs.

BRANSGORE, THE CROWN INN c1960 B695010

BURLEY, THE VILLAGE C1950 B647016

Many of the present buildings in Burley are Victorian and 20th-century, but the village itself is an ancient Forest settlement. People have certainly lived here since the Iron Age - a fortification from that period on Burley Beacon Ridge guards the surrounding heathland.

BURLEY, THE VILLAGE C1955 B647012

Once a lonely hamlet in the Forest, beloved of smugglers and witches, Burley's residents were once said to depend on the annual crop of 'akermast' - acorns and mast.

BURLEY
The Village c1955 B647015
Not far away from the village are local
quarries where a kind of gravel
called Burley Rock was excavated in
earlier times. This material was used
for the foundations of a number
of New Forest churches.

BURLEY, THE VILLAGE c1955 B647017

In the early years of the 20th century, the colourful Auberon Herbert lived near Burley. Herbert was an aristocrat, politician, republican and writer. He acquired fame and affection for the mouth-watering tea-parties he gave for local villagers, children and New Forest gypsies.

BURLEY, MANOR FARM TEA GARDENS c1960 B647028

Sir Walter Scott, poet and novelist, visited Burley and compared favourably the wild heathland thereabouts to his beloved Scottish border countryside.

BURLEY, THE CROSS AND THE POST OFFICE c1960 B647032

During the 20th century Burley grew considerably in size, with a number of villa-style residences tucked away among the trees and heathlands. It has never lost its village atmosphere.

BURLEY, THE VILLAGE c1960 B647062

Despite its increase in size, Burley is still a good centre for exploring the southwestern corner of the New Forest, with lonely woodlands and heaths within easy walking distance. The naturalist can see foxes, badgers, deer and a huge variety of birdlife in the immediate vicinity.

BURLEY, THE MANOR HOTEL c1960 B647001

BURLEY
The Manor Hotel c1960
Tourism in the New Forest is really a 20th-century phenomenon. An earlier trickle of visitors has now given way to something of a torrent, though increased numbers have not diminished the attractiveness of the setting. A number of older houses became hotels in the last century to cope with the increased demand.

◆

BURLEY
Flying G Ranch c1960
A thatched farmhouse in the New Forest - an unlikely setting for a ranch dedicated to the memory and horse-riding style of the Wild West. But that is what this old building became in the middle of the 20th century.

BURLEY, FLYING G RANCH c1960 B647042

BURLEY, FLYING G RANCH c1955 B647302

Here we see visitors hitting the trail. The popularity of Western books, films and television programmes in the 1950s and 1960s lured many would-be cowboys to this Wild West of the New Forest.

BURLEY, FLYING G RANCH c1960 B647047

Two identical cowgirls and a dog on a sunny day at the Flying G Ranch. This scene could almost have come from some remote spot in the American west.

CADNAM, TWIN OAKS 1932 85061

Cadnam, or Cadenham, stands at an important road junction at the north-western corner of the New Forest; sooner or later every traveller in the locality is bound to pass through the village. The site would have been well-known two thousand years ago - a Roman road ran nearby.

CADNAM, THE SIR JOHN BARLEYCORN INN 1932 85062

In the 1930s the Sir John Barleycorn Inn was just one of several taverns in the Cadnam area - known only to locals, visitors from nearby towns, and passing travellers.

CADNAM, THE SIR JOHN BARLEYCORN INN c1960 C3011
Thirty years later the Sir John Barleycorn Inn had achieved its present popularity, drawing in visitors from further afield. As a comparison between the two photographs shows, the inn had changed little in the intervening years.

CADNAM, THE SIR WALTER TYRRELL c1960 C3011
Named after the knight who killed William Rufus, the Sir Walter Tyrrell became another hostelry that achieved prominence during the age of popular motoring - as this full car park indicates.

CADNAM
The Green c1960
Cadnam's extensive green is yet another
of those delightful wide open spaces that
seem to always be in close proximity to
so many New Forest villages. The
straggling geese draw the eye naturally
into this charming scene.

◆

CADNAM
The Forest Stores and Post Office c1960
Many visitors made their way to Cadnam
to view the celebrated oak tree that buds
in midwinter. Tradition says that the
harder the winter, the more leaves
that appear.

CADNAM, THE GREEN c1960 C3024

CADNAM, THE FOREST STORES AND POST OFFICE c1960 C3041

DIBDEN PURLIEU, THE VILLAGE c1960 D196007

This is a thoroughly 20th-century building in the very ancient village of Dibden. The village stands on the edge of the Forest overlooking Southampton Water. Its church is some eight centuries old, and its altar rails are made from an even older yew tree that once stood in the churchyard.

EMERY DOWN, THE CHURCH 1892 31392

Not far from Lyndhurst is the village of Emery Down, blessed with a number of attractive cottages and a row of quite beautiful almshouses. Its church was built and endowed by Admiral Boultbee, who lies buried in the churchyard.

EMERY DOWN, THE VILLAGE 1904 51463
Emery Down stands on the frontier of some of the wildest scenery in the New Forest. Badgers live deep in the woods, deer can be seen by the patient watcher, and buzzards circle overhead.

EMERY DOWN, THE GREEN 1904 51464
Cattle graze on Emery Down's green in the early years of the last century, a more familiar sight then than now. By the end of the 20th century the village had become a rural suburb of nearby Lyndhurst.

EMERY DOWN, THE VILLAGE c1955 E196006

Emery Down, like many old Forest settlements, has seen its share of England's history. Roman legions marched this way on the nearby Roman roads, Norman huntsmen chased the deer through the nearby woodlands and Civil War soldiers skirmished on the nearby heathlands.

EMERY DOWN, THE POST OFFICE c1955 E196010

The roads of the New Forest tend to be much busier these days than they were when this photograph was taken. The best way to explore the Forest is to use a village such as Emery Down as a base and then explore on foot or horseback.

EMERY DOWN, THE SWAN INN C1960 E196013
The New Forest has some of the best public houses in southern England, whether the visitor is seeking accommodation or just calling in for a tasty lunch and a drink after a hard morning's walk.

EMERY DOWN, THE NEW FOREST INN C1960 E196019
The New Forest Inn is another popular hostelry at Emery Down. In previous centuries the old taverns hereabouts were much used by smugglers, who had brought into the Forest the contraband they had landed on the south coast.

EMERY DOWN
The Church c1960

This final view over Emery Down shows the extent to which the deep woodlands of the New Forest cluster around this ancient settlement. This wildness has survived into the 21st century.

◆

HINTON
The Cat and Fiddle 1900

The famous Cat and Fiddle Inn at Hinton Admiral is some seven hundred years old. In recent years this public house has become a favourite trip for tourists staying in nearby Christchurch and Bournemouth.

EMERY DOWN, THE CHURCH c1960 E196033

HINTON, THE CAT AND FIDDLE 1900 45058

IBSLEY, THE BRIDGE 1890 24074

The bridge over the River Avon at Ibsley, with its white water weir, wildfowl and waterside scenery, is a good place to halt if you are following that lovely river up from the sea. Napoleonic prisoners-of-war planted an avenue of elm trees here, which survived until the devastation of 20th-century road widening.

IBSLEY, THE OLD BEAMS c1955 I55003

Former inhabitants of Ibsley must have been generous souls. Early church registers reveal that collections were made 'towards the redemption of the poor slaves out of Turkey', 'for the redemption of all captives' and 'for the distressed Protestants beyond the sea'.

LINWOOD, THE VILLAGE c1965 L508007
Linwood is situated high on the heathlands of the western edge of the New Forest, overlooking the broad valley of the Avon. It is one of the most isolated villages in the locality; its lonely open road winds across the heart of King William's old hunting territory.

NEW MILTON, OLD MILTON CHURCH c1965 N58009
Milton's church tower is nearly four hundred years old, though the rest of the building is more recent. Inside is a monument to the soldier Thomas White, who died in 1720 after faithful service to four monarchs.

NEW MILTON
The Parade 1910 N58001
Milton, Old and New, is now a sprawling suburb near to Highcliffe and Christchurch. The village lost half a hyde of land and its woodlands to the hunting forest, according to the Domesday Book, though rents were halved by way of compensation.

NEW MILTON, THATCHED COTTAGE c1965 N58020
The cliffs south of Milton are renowned for the profusion of fossils to be found. Examples can be seen in local museums and at the Natural History Museum in London.

PILLEY, THE VILLAGE AND THE GREEN 1955 P285001
The little village of Pilley lies to the west of Beaulieu Heath, above the low-lying ground surrounding the Beaulieu River. By taking one of the several bridleways in this area it is still quite possible to get away from the noise and bustle of the 21st century.

PILLEY, THE POST OFFICE C1955 P285003
Pilley is a short stroll from Boldre on an ancient route to the vast expanse of Beaulieu Heath. Along this route would have passed kings of England on their way to hunt, medieval travellers on pilgrimages to Beaulieu Abbey, and generations of drovers with their herds of livestock on the way to long-established grazing grounds.

SOPLEY, THE CHURCH 1900 45064
Standing on a little hilltop, Sopley Church overlooks the course of the Avon. The building was established in 1270; just inside the doorway are stone carvings of the local squire and his wife, who endowed this lovely place of worship.

SOPLEY, THE VILLAGE 1900 45063
Sopley probably gets its name from soc leag: land granted the right to hold a court of socmen. The sign above the inn says that Louisa Brinson is 'licensed to sell beer, wines, spirits and tobacco'.

SWAY, THE PARISH CHURCH OF ST LUKE c1955 S638016

Sway stands on the high road between Brockenhurst and Bournemouth, and is dominated by a concrete tower built by a Mr Peterson. Some say it was built as a tomb or cenotaph, others as a simple demonstration of the durability of concrete.

SWAY, THE CHURCH AND THE SCHOOL c1955 S638013

Tradition alleges that Mr Peterson incurred the wrath of the Admiralty for putting a light at the top of his tower. Naval captains complained that their ships were mistaking the tower for a lighthouse as they navigated up the Solent.

SWAY, THE POST OFFICE c1955 S638022

Given its proximity to the seaside towns of Lymington and Christchurch, Sway became a popular place to live during the 20th century. Not all the original locals were happy with the spread of villa residences. But most of these newer buildings have now blended in with the background.

SWAY, THE HARE AND HOUNDS c1955 S638018

On the heathlands above Sway are the burial grounds of early man. Buckland Rings, the great earthworks nearby, probably date back to the Iron Age, though the Romans used the fortifications during their invasion of England - coins of the Emperor Claudius have been found within its defensive banks.

SWAY

The Forest Heath Hotel c1955

Sway is a good centre for visitors to the New Forest who wish to explore the southern coastline without staying in a busy resort. A number of inns, hotels and bed and breakfast establishments cater for the tourist.

◆

SWAY

The Post Office c1955

The local shop can be as important to the social life of a village community as the public house. It is not just a place to buy groceries or post a letter, but a place to catch up on all the local gossip - or a place to meet old friends.

SWAY, THE FOREST HEATH HOTEL c1955 S638021

SWAY, THE POST OFFICE c1955 S638024

FOUR NEW FOREST TOWNS

WITH THE LARGER settlements of the New Forest, it is hard to know just where a village ends and a town begins. Brockenhurst, Fordingbridge, Lyndhurst and Ringwood are not very big compared to towns elsewhere in southern England; but all are bigger than the villages nearby, and all four are important as far as the history of the New Forest goes.

Brockenhurst derives its name from the landscape that surrounds it, being Anglo-Saxon for badger's wood. Its church, standing on a high mound overlooking its cottages, is one of only two New Forest churches to be mentioned in the Domesday Book. Though much of this building is Norman and Early English, there has been quite an amount of restoration, some of it unfortunate, though time has mellowed the worst excesses of its restorers. The scenery hereabouts can be quite idyllic, particularly when the traffic has died down, with its shadowing woodlands and wide open lawns where animals graze and walkers linger. Brockenhurst grew considerably during the 20th century thanks to its convenient railway connections and close proximity to larger centres of population. It says a lot for the capacity of the

New Forest to absorb new buildings that the setting was not altogether compromised or the town ruined.

Away to the north-west corner of the Forest is the town of Fordingbridge. This too is a community named after its geographical situation, for it sprawls around a very ancient crossing point over the River Avon. The landscape round about is pastoral, all hedgerows and flood meadows, a sharp contrast to the wilder countryside to the east. In earlier days the village was known as Forde, and the lord of the manor was obliged to mount a watch on its bridge to stop suspected persons from leaving the Forest. As is typical with a settlement at a river crossing, Fordingbridge has a long history; fording places were of great importance before the bridge-building sprees of medieval times. At nearby Castle Hill is a hill-fort used successively by Iron Age warriors, Roman soldiers and Saxon chieftains.

Lyndhurst, 'lime wood' in Old English, stands roughly at the centre of the New Forest, and deserves its title as the Forest's capital. William the Conqueror held this manor for himself during his tenure as Master of the

Forest. It is here that the Verderers' Court has met since Norman times to regulate the Forest, uphold the Forest Laws and arbitrate in local disputes. Lyndhurst's church is Victorian, though occupying an older site, while the rest of the town is one long and not particularly ancient street. In recent years it has had its detractors, critical of the town's almost total commitment to the tourist trade. But it has admirers as well, for a short walk in any direction takes the stroller away from the bustle and traffic and into the heart of the Forest glades and wildest of heathland.

Ringwood stands on the Avon, near to the boundary between the New Forest and Ringwood Forest, its name meaning either a village on the edge of a forest or a river crossing point. Either description is very appropriate, for Ringwood has all the feeling of a border town, though it has increased in size considerably and become lightly industrialised during the 20th century The town prospered even in Victorian times - as did so many others - because of the coming of a railway line, which in this case connected Ringwood to the south coast and London. Unfortunately, the railway is no more, and Ringwood has to contend with an increasing amount of traffic as it enters the 21st century. Even in the last century the town sacrificed its delightful old corn mill and its vicarage for the benefit of the motor car.

These four towns are good bases for exploring the surrounding countryside, being nicely spaced out around the New Forest. A few days spent in each of them in turn, quartering the Forest on foot, or horseback, or pedal cycle, would be an excellent introduction to all of the places captured on film by the Frith photographers.

RINGWOOD, FRIDAY'S CROSS c1955 R35023

BROCKENHURST, THE VILLAGE c1955 B394006

The village of Brockenhurst lies in one of the most attractive parts of the New Forest, and many of its cottages are of considerable antiquity. Given the ease of access by car and train, it makes an excellent centre for an exploration of the southern half of the Forest.

BROCKENHURST, THE VILLAGE c1955 B394001

Near to the village are the extensive grounds of Brockenhurst Park, the home of the Morant family until well into the last century. Nine hundred years earlier the estate was held by the Spelman family on condition that they provided a bed for the king and hay for his horse if he visited Brockenhurst.

BROCKENHURST, THE RAILWAY CROSSING c1955 B394008
Brockenhurst is a railway junction well-known to travellers to Southampton, Bournemouth, Lymington and the Isle of Wight. Some of those who work in the first three places have chosen to make their homes in this charming little town.

BROCKENHURST, THE CHURCH c1960 B394014
Brockenhurst's parish church is a beautiful building, showing both Norman and Early English styles of architecture. The church is dedicated to St Nicholas, patron saint of wayfarers and children. In the churchyard is the grave of 'Brusher' Mills, the famous New Forest snake-catcher.

BROCKENHURST, BALMER LAWN c1960 B394016

BROCKENHURST
Balmer Lawn c1960
Balmer Lawn is a popular picnic spot situated to the north-west of Brockenhurst. The lawns around the town are areas originally cleared of woodland, both to provide timber and to allow deer to graze.

FORDINGBRIDGE
The Bridge c1960
To the north-west of the New Forest is the peaceful little town of Fordingbridge, named after the ancient ford and medieval bridge which facilitate a passage across the River Avon at this point. The bridge, built originally in the 14th century, is now a scheduled ancient monument.

FORDINGBRIDGE, THE BRIDGE c1960 F178009

FORDINGBRIDGE, BRIDGE STREET c1960 F178023

In earlier days this route marked the only highway in and out of the Forest from this direction. During the period of 'Fence Month' - fifteen days either side of midsummer - the lord of the manor was instructed by to keep a watch on the bridge and challenge anyone entering or leaving the New Forest.

FORDINGBRIDGE, HIGH STREET c1960 F178006

Fordingbridge is now a busy market town, though in former days it was an important industrial centre, renowned for the manufacture of sailcloth and canvas. Today it is popular with tourists who wish to explore the New Forest and the downlands of Dorset.

FORDINGBRIDGE, HIGH STREET c1960 F178026
In very early times Fordingbridge was known simply as 'Forde', a crossing point of the Avon since prehistoric times. A hospital dedicated to St John existed here during medieval times, until its dissolution during the reign of Henry VIII.

FORDINGBRIDGE, THE CHURCH c1965 F178050
The church of St Mary is Early English in style and some eight hundred years old. The Lady Chapel shows off medieval craftsmanship at its best, its roof adorned with carvings of biblical prophets, clusters of flowers and even the head of God, enveloped in clouds.

FORDINGBRIDGE, THE CHURCH c1960 F178008
There is a sad epitaph to John Chubb in the churchyard, who died young in 1784: 'Death like an overflowing stream sweeps us away: Our life's a dream: An empty tale: A morning flower cut down and withered in an hour'.

FORDINGBRIDGE, TOWN CENTRE c1960 F178056
The Domesday Book records that the manor of Fordingbridge possessed a church and two mills, and was rented at 14s 2d. Though all of its woodlands, formerly used for pannage (grazing by swine), were taken for use by the Conqueror as hunting land, the villagers received no reduction in rent.

FORDINGBRIDGE, STREET SCENE c1960 F178019
People have lived in the vicinity of Fordingbridge for millennia. Not far away at Castle Hill is a hillfort dating back to the Iron Age. Roman, Anglo-Saxon and Danish warriors would all have known this neighbourhood.

LYNDHURST, THE STREET 1890 24080
Travelling north along the straight road from Brockenhurst brings the traveller to Lyndhurst, an ideal centre for exploring the northern edges of the great forest. Notice how Mr Short, the chemist on the left, had diversified into photography - a favourite hobby at the time.

LYNDHURST, THE CROWN HOTEL 1890 24079
The Crown Hotel, formerly one of Lyndhurst's inns, was rebuilt in the Tudor style late in Victoria's reign to cater for those who came to delight in the beauties of the New Forest.

LYNDHURST, THE CHURCH 1891 29589
For such an old town, the church of St Michael and All Angels is modern, being built as recently as 1860 over the site of an older church and a 13th-century chapel. In the churchyard is the grave of Mrs Reginald Hargreaves, born Alice Liddell and immortalised by Lewis Carroll in 'Alice in Wonderland'.

LYNDHURST, THE STAG INN 1890 24082

Standing at the junction of several ancient roads, Lyndhurst has attracted travellers for centuries. Many of the town's inns would have been established for these traditional wayfarers. Now they cater for the thousands of tourists who use Lyndhurst as a base for touring the New Forest.

LYNDHURST, HIGH STREET 1897 40568

Lyndhurst's main street runs from east to west, dominated by the church on the higher ground at one end. Much of the administrative work of the New Forest is carried out here. Five times a year the Verderers meet here to discuss important Forest business.

LYNDHURST, THE CROWN HOTEL 1897 40571

LYNDHURST
The Crown Hotel **1897**
That great huntsman William I held the
manor of Lyndhurst in his own hands
after the land around was taken in as a
hunting forest. The old forest laws
applied after the Conquest were cruel,
and many of the original inhabitants
would have suffered appalling injustices.

◆

LYNDHURST
The Crown Hotel **1897**
Lyndhurst is known as the capital of the
New Forest, with the ancient hunting
ground lying all around. The town's
name comes from Old English and
means lime or linden wood. Domesday
Book calls the settlement here Linhest.

LYNDHURST, THE CROWN HOTEL 1897 40570

LYNDHURST, ENTRANCE TO THE TOWN 1900 46106

In early days the royal manor of Lyndhurst was often granted to the queens of England. Henry III gave it to Eleanor of Castile, the wife of Edward I. It was subsequently held by Margaret of France, Isabella - the wife of Edward II - and Philippa of Hainault.

LYNDHURST, KING'S HOUSE 1904 51462

The kings of England often used Lyndhurst as a base for their hunting expeditions in the New Forest. The King's House dates from 1640, though it has been much restored. The old hunting forest was surrendered by Queen Victoria, so that more people could enjoy its delights.

LYNDHURST
Shrubs Hill Cottage 1906

There are many charming cottages in the vicinity of Lyndhurst, some of them probably dating back to the 13th century when the harsh forest laws were relaxed somewhat during the reign of Henry III.

◆

LYNDHURST
High Street 1908

This is a revealing picture of changing times. Towards the end of the Edwardian period the horses and carriages available for hire at the Stag Hotel faced competition from the motor cars for hire from the neighbouring Imperial Garage.

LYNDHURST, SHRUBS HILL COTTAGE 1906   55892

LYNDHURST, HIGH STREET 1908   60105

LYNDHURST
High Street 1908 60104
By Edwardian times Lyndhurst's shops were catering for
something of a tourist boom. Several establishments are seen
here offering refreshments. The Frith photographer may have
had some competition, for the chemist on the left has a wide
selection of photographic materials on sale.

LYNDHURST, HIGH STREET 1908 60106

A fine example of a traditional Edwardian shop front. Misselbrook and Weston's provision store seems to have offered every grocery product the discerning customer could desire. The ironmonger across the road offers all that a Forest dweller might need.

LYNDHURST, STREET SCENE 1908 60107

The coming of the railway in Victoria's time had made Lyndhurst very popular, though George III had resided there a century earlier. Artists such as Millais and Leighton sought inspiration in local scenes, and a host of Victorian and Edwardian amateurs followed their example.

LYNDHURST
High Street 1934

The coming of the motor car made Lyndhurst a much busier place, as can be observed by comparing this view with earlier photographs of the same location. With the advent of popular motoring from the 1950s onwards, the presence of hundreds of cars on summer days threatened to engulf the little town.

◆

LYNDHURST
The Crown Hotel c1955

By the 1950s the Crown Hotel had become a favoured halt for car-borne tourists, offering meals as well as accommodation. By this time the Crown had received the prestigious approval of the Automobile Association and the Royal Automobile Club - as the signs confirm.

LYNDHURST, HIGH STREET 1934 86279

LYNDHURST, THE CROWN HOTEL c1955 L123026

LYNDHURST, NEW FOREST PONIES c1955 L123011

LYNDHURST
New Forest Ponies c1955
The famous New Forest ponies remind us that Lyndhurst is very much a Forest town. Sometimes the inhabitants of the Forest, whether they be ponies, deer, badger or foxes, still come to town.

◆

LYNDHURST
The Grand Hotel c1955
There are many wide open spaces around Lyndhurst, where the Forest meets the town. They are good places for a stroll if the depths of the old hunting forest are too daunting. From this one there are fine views over the town.

LYNDHURST, THE GRAND HOTEL c1955 L123039

LYNDHURST, THE DONKEYS c1955 L123025

Two donkeys make friends with some passing visitors, probably hoping to cadge a snack or two. Feeding the animals in the Forest is now strictly forbidden, as a number of animals have been run down by cars after having been lured to the roadside.

LYNDHURST, PONIES ON THE GREEN, CADNAM ROAD c1955 L123055

This is a lovely study of two New Forest ponies on the approaches to Lyndhurst. The northwards journey to Cadnam goes through exquisite forest scenery and a variety of wildlife can be seen if the car is left behind.

LYNDHURST, SWAN GREEN C1955 L123035

You cannot leave Lyndhurst in any direction without going through some of the best parts of the New Forest. Swan Green is just one such place not far away, where it is possible to enjoy a peaceful picnic under the shade of a stately tree.

RINGWOOD, MARKET PLACE 1890 24055

Ringwood stands on the banks of the meandering River Avon, at the New Forest's western boundary. A Saxon town in origin, it may get its name from its location. Its name is either derived from Rincrede, a river crossing point, or Rimucwude, meaning the edge of the forest. The Domesday Book refers to the settlement as Rinwede.

RINGWOOD, THE FISH INN FROM THE MARKET PLACE 1890 24053
Ringwood's houses date from most periods of England's history and include some modern buildings - for this is both a commuter town and a favourite place for retirement. Notice the antiquated tricycle just behind the taller of the two ladders.

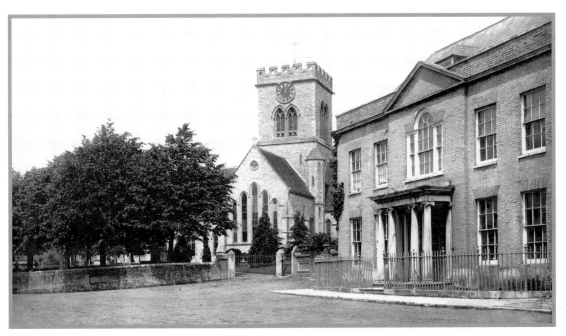

RINGWOOD, THE CHURCH FROM THE MARKET PLACE 1890 24061
Ringwood's parish church dated originally to the 13th century, but suffered so badly at the hands of restorers that it had to be rebuilt in Early English style in 1854 - fortunately a number of features from the earlier building were retained.

RINGWOOD, THE CONGREGATIONAL CHAPEL 1890 24060

Too many visitors to England's country towns content themselves with a visit to only the parish church. To do so is to miss a great deal of interesting architecture, such as Ringwood's striking 19th-century congregational chapel.

RINGWOOD, AVON CASTLE 1891 28650

Avon Castle, on the opposite bank of the river from Ringwood, is an area that has become increasingly built-up and urbanised since this photograph of a country gentleman's home was taken in the last full decade of Queen Victoria's reign.

RINGWOOD
Somerley House 1891

To the north-west of Ringwood is Somerley House, sometime residence of Lord Normanton. In the valley to the east are the winding waters of the River Avon, to the west the trees of Ringwood Forest.

RINGWOOD
The Millstream 1900

King Henry III granted Ringwood a market charter in 1226, which was confirmed by Edward VI in 1553. Ringwood's market brought country folk from far and wide to the town with their goods; it also became famous for the sale of New Forest ponies.

RINGWOOD, SOMERLEY HOUSE 1891 28651

RINGWOOD, THE MILLSTREAM 1900 45026

RINGWOOD, THE MILLSTREAM 1900 45027

A fine view over the River Avon, with a horse cooling itself by the ancient ford and a thatcher practising his age-old craft on one of Ringwood's most picturesque cottages.

RINGWOOD, THE MILLSTREAM 1900 45032

According to Domesday Book, Ringwood's mill was quite profitable, paying 22s in revenue. Before William's invasion this land was held by Earl Tostig, but four hydes of land from the original ten were seized for the creation of the Norman hunting forest.

RINGWOOD, THE MILL AND THE CHURCH 1900 45031

The River Avon is famous for a rare kind of eel, called locally a sniggle; unlike the Common Eel, it has an elongated jaw and slender form. It would probably have been a staple part of the diet of early Ringwood residents.

RINGWOOD, HIGH STREET 1900 45036

On the right hand side of the High Street is the White Hart Inn. It was probably here that the Duke of Monmouth was brought as a prisoner following the crushing of his rebellion in 1685. During his brief stay Monmouth wrote letters to his uncle James II pleading for mercy - but in vain. Monmouth was beheaded soon afterwards in the Tower of London.

RINGWOOD, CHRISTCHURCH STREET 1900 45033

RINGWOOD
Christchurch Street 1900
Another resident at this time was Lady Alice Lisle, who allegedly offered shelter to some of Monmouth's rebels. The notorious Judge Jeffries condemned her to be burned at the stake, but this sentence was commuted to beheading. She is buried in the nearby churchyard at Ellingham.

◆

RINGWOOD
Southampton Street 1913
Over the centuries a number of inns were established in Ringwood, many brewing a variety of local ales. One local gardener, a certain Mr Blower, was renowned for his ability to drink sixteen pints of the local ale in a day.

RINGWOOD, SOUTHAMPTON STREET 1913 65632

RINGWOOD, COXSTONE LANE 1913 65639

A Victorian entrepreneur Charles Castleman fought hard to bring a railway to Ringwood in the 1840s. The town eventually became a station on the London to Dorchester line. Given the lack of straight sections of line in the vicinity, the railway here was nicknamed 'Castleman's Corkscrew'. The railway exists no longer, though even in 1913 older forms of transport survived.

RINGWOOD, FRIDAY'S CROSS c1955 R35023

By the 1950s the town of Ringwood began to grow dramatically, being within commuting distance of places of employment such as Bournemouth. Light industry came to Ringwood, offering employment at a time of decline in agriculture and traditional crafts.

RINGWOOD, THE MARKET SQUARE c1955 R35026
A pedal cyclist rides through the deserted site of Ringwood's ancient market. The growth of popular motoring was to lead to the destruction of Ringwood's old corn mill, and even its vicarage, to facilitate the movement of traffic.

RINGWOOD, WEST STREET c1955 R35045
Ringwood makes an excellent centre for touring the New Forest, Ringwood Forest, the Dorset downlands and even the south coast. A number of its buildings are now used for the antiques trade or to provide refreshment. Half a century ago this delightful thatched cottage combined the two.

RINGWOOD
Old Cottage Tea Rooms c1965
It is ten years after photograph No R35045, and still this lovely building serves tea to an appreciative clientele. An increasing number of Hampshire's most beautiful buildings were used for this refreshing purpose during the 20th century.

RINGWOOD
The Kettle Tea House, Picket Post c1955
Picket Post is a tiny hamlet on the high road between Ringwood and the New Forest. It is a convenient place to stop for tea, sit on a bench and watch the world go by.

RINGWOOD, OLD COTTAGE TEA ROOMS c1965 R35119

RINGWOOD, THE KETTLE TEA HOUSE, PICKET POST c1955 R35069

THE COASTAL FRINGE

AT FIRST GLANCE the coast between Bournemouth and Southampton may seem to have little to do with the New Forest, which now begins a mile or two into the interior of Hampshire. But a thousand years ago, the bounds of William the Conqueror's great hunting forest were drawn more widely than the reduced boundary of today. Many of these coastal communities have had some connection with the Forest over the centuries. They may have acted as its ports, used its timber for shipbuilding or provided Forest residents with food and merchants' goods. These days, of course, many visitors to the New Forest choose to stay in places such as Bournemouth, Christchurch or Lymington.

For the Norman kings hunting deer in the depths of the New Forest, the site of what is now Bournemouth, if they had known of it at all, would have been familiar only as wild and windswept heathland. No known house stood there until Mr Lewis Tregonwell built a holiday home as recently as 1810. Many others followed his example, and by the end of the 19th century the town had become a most popular resort to which thousands of holidaymakers flocked each year. It is now a university town, and has achieved city status - and all within two hundred years. Although it is now in neighbouring Dorset, its visitors make regular trips into Hampshire to seek out the wild heaths and ancient woodlands of the New Forest.

Christchurch is as old as Bournemouth is new, for the Romans are known to have settled at Hengistbury Head; they probably used the shelter of what is now Christchurch harbour as a port for trading vessels and war galleys. Its priory church was built by the Normans on the site of an earlier Saxon foundation, and happens to be the longest parish church in England. The town that clusters around it is a delight, full of lovely old buildings in a wide variety of architectural styles and periods. Christchurch is as good a base as any for an exploration of the New Forest.

Lymington has often served as a Forest port; it has an honourable mention in Domesday Book, which records that a small hamlet stood here. Domesday records a 120-acre farm at nearby Woodside as being of more value than the rest of the settlement put together. One Roger de Yvery held one hyde of land here, but the old manor received a rate reduction of a half on the account of its woods being taken into the Forest. By 1345 Lymington had grown to such size and power that it could afford to send more ships to aid Edward III's invasion of France than Portsmouth.

Boats leave Lymington daily to cross the Solent to the Isle of Wight. Some tourists head in the other direction, taking the high road to Brockenhurst or across Beaulieu heath into some of the most scenic areas of the New Forest.

The few miles of coast running eastwards of Lymington is little known to most tourists until the estuary of the Beaulieu River is reached. Half way up this enchanting stretch of water is the picturesque hamlet of Bucklers Hard - the inspiration for a thousand picture postcard photographers. Yet two centuries ago this quiet backwater had its own industry - shipbuilding. Many men-o'-war of Nelson's time were laid down here, including the 'Agamemnon', one of the great admiral's favourite commands. Three of the vessels built here by the Adams brothers fought at Trafalgar. Yet the enterprise failed when the company was late delivering four ships to the Admiralty. Now Bucklers Hard is the haunt of the leisure yachting fraternity and the day-tripper.

A further turn of the coast, past the little hamlet of Lepe - another place with Roman connections - brings us to the busy estuary of Southampton Water and access to one of the world's most important maritime ports. Its western banks have been transformed by the oil industry into a landscape that seems alien to the beauty and tranquillity of the nearby New Forest. Yet look beneath the industrial surface of places like Fawley and Hythe and history is waiting to be found.

Tradition states that the Saxon warlord Cerdic landed at Fawley to begin his colonisation of what was to become Wessex. Fawley was a substantial village at the time of the Norman Conquest, when it was absorbed into William's Forest; it was still relatively unspoiled in the earlier years of the 20th century. Hythe, now a large and busy community, was once the port of the New Forest; because of this status it survived the worst excesses of the Conqueror's predations. Though both communities are now urbanised, a short walk will bring the traveller to the wilder countryside of the New Forest: it reminds us that nature has the power to resist even humanity's tendency to urbanise and develop the landscape.

KEYHAVEN, THE WATERSIDE c1960 K146038

BARTON-ON-SEA, THE SANDS c1960 B690025
Here we see a traditional donkey ride - a familiar treat on a 20th-century seaside holiday. Barton-on-Sea enjoys a sandy setting on the shores of Christchurch Bay, just across from the Isle of Wight.

BARTON-ON-SEA, THE CLIFFS c1960 B690040
Geologically the cliffs at Barton-on-Sea are very colourful, not unlike those across the Solent on the Isle of Wight. The area around is rich hunting territory for the collector of fossils.

BOURNEMOUTH, BOSCOBEL TOWER 1887 19544

Bournemouth was a late starter as a seaside resort, for the land on which it stands was just wild and windswept heath until Mr Lewis Tregonwell built a holiday home there in 1810. By 1890, when this photograph was taken, the population had grown to over 30,000.

BOURNEMOUTH, THE GARDENS 1890 25502

Victorian Bournemouth was a most fashionable place, which had the advantage over older resorts of developing purely for a burgeoning holiday industry. A vacation in Bournemouth became a childhood memory for millions of young Britons during the 20th century.

BOURNEMOUTH, THE PIER ENTRANCE 1900 45213
By the last year of Victoria's reign Bournemouth had become an established seaside resort. Apart from the grand pier there were public baths and a subscription reading room - all shown in this photograph.

BUCKLERS HARD, THE VILLAGE c1960 B43044
Halfway down the estuary of the Beaulieu river stands the little community of Bucklers Hard. During the great days of sail many men-o'-war were built here, including the 'Agamemnon', the 'Bellerophon' and the 'Illustrious'. The hamlet declined in importance with the advent of the warships.

BUCKLERS HARD, THE VILLAGE c1960 B43045

The 'Agamemnon' was launched here in 1781, a powerful 1400 tons carrying 64 guns. Horatio Nelson, who commanded here, was wont to remark that she was the finest 64-gunner in the fleet; he fought some of his earliest naval battles in that remarkable ship.

BUCKLERS HARD, THE VILLAGE c1960 B43024

Using local timber from the woodlands along the estuary, the shipbuilders of Bucklers Hard, who would have lived in these cottages, built at least three of the ships which fought at the Battle of Trafalgar in 1805.

BUCKLERS HARD, THE CHAPEL AND HOSTEL c1960 B43046
The Beaulieu River, being a free harbour, attracted the attentions of John, Duke of Montagu in the 18th century as a trading centre for the sugar trade and shipbuilding. The first vessel to be launched here was the 14-gun 'Surprise'.

BUCKLERS HARD, THE VILLAGE c1960 B43043
The Master Builder's House, now an hotel, was built by Henry Adams so that he might cut a dash on ship-launching days. In those days, when piles of seasoning timber would line the streets, Adams entertained two kings of England in his house. The business failed when Adams and his brother were late building four ships for the Admiralty.

BUCKLERS HARD, THE VILLAGE C1960 B43025

Although a fair distance from the present limits of the New Forest, Bucklers Hard was certainly within its boundaries at the time of William the Conqueror - there may well have been a small settlement here at the time.

BUCKLERS HARD, YACHTS C1960 B43075

Bucklers Hard and the Beaulieu River are now visited regularly by yachtsmen who are fond of the old anchorage. The boats of today would have seemed modest in size moored alongside the men-o'-war of Nelson's navy.

BUCKLERS HARD, NEW FOREST PONIES c1960 B43063

Ponies graze on the wide open spaces around Bucklers Hard, a reminder that the New Forest and its surrounding heathlands are never far away from the shores and estuaries of the south coast.

CHRISTCHURCH, THE PRIORY CHURCH 1890 25203

Christchurch is one of the oldest settlements around the New Forest. It was probably in existence even before the Romans settled in the shelter of Hengistbury Head after 43 AD. It owes its continued existence to the patronage of Saxon kings and its later adoption by the Normans.

CHRISTCHURCH, THE PRIORY 1900 45040

An earlier Saxon church was demolished by the Normans in 1095. The present building, the longest parish church in England, was built in its place. Legend tells us that a mysterious carpenter aided its construction, and the building was named Christchurch in his honour.

CHRISTCHURCH, HIGH STREET 1900 45043A

Christchurch's High Street boasts much fine Georgian and Victorian architecture. Leading up to the castle and priory church, the High Street has always been the focus of the town. It is interesting to remember that trade prospered in this street for centuries before a single house was built in neighbouring Bournemouth.

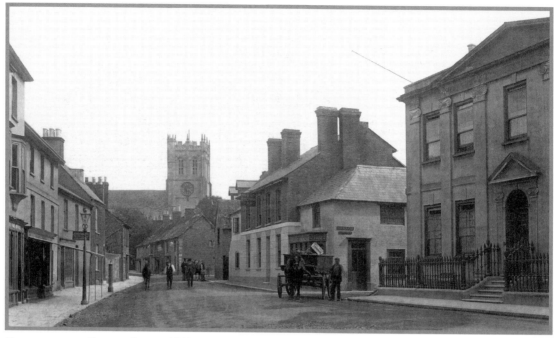

CHRISTCHURCH, CHURCH STREET 1900 45053

This view shows a working community and this old town still thrives today. Until around this time fishing was still a major industry in Christchurch, though its port never really developed beyond the present simple harbour.

CHRISTCHURCH, WICK FERRY 1900 45044

Christchurch stands on two rivers, the Stour and the Avon. The town gets its old name of Twyneham from the Anglo-Saxon, meaning 'the town between two rivers'. The rivers are very popular for boating and their banks are an ideal site for a picnic.

CHRISTCHURCH
Wick Ferry 1900
Even in 1900 tourists were flocking to such picturesque places as this on foot, in boats, and on bicycles. Larger crowds now throng the estuary on hot summer days.

◆

CHRISTCHURCH
Blackwater Ferry 1900
An ancient rope-pulled ferry crosses the River Stour at Blackwater. In Saxon times, before many bridges were built, rivers formed real obstacles to travel, and ferries thrived.

CHRISTCHURCH, WICK FERRY 1900 45045

CHRISTCHURCH, BLACKWATER FERRY 1900 45048

CHRISTCHURCH, THE RIVER STOUR 1918 68054

The circular estuary of the Stour and Avon, where the two rivers penetrate far inland, and the shores of Christchurch Bay, attract thousands of sea and wading birds, particularly during the winter months - a joy for the birdwatcher.

CHRISTCHURCH, THE RIVER BANK 1918 68052

In the year 901 the Saxon Ethelwald held the castle in rebellion against his kinsman Edward the Elder. The older Saxon church of Holy Trinity then dominated the harbour scenery. The present church was begun at the end of the 11th century by the Norman cleric Roger Flambard.

CHRISTCHURCH, THE BOWLING GREEN AND CASTLE RUINS c1955 C99099
The ruins of Christchurch's Norman castle dominate the town much less than the church of the same period. The castle was built by Roger de Redvers in the 12th century. Today its shadow falls on peaceful pursuits such as a game of bowls.

FAWLEY, ASHLETT CREEK c1955 F150031
Fawley stands on the western bank of Southampton Water, just where it flows out into the Solent. Ancient heathland surrounds the landward side of the village, but much of its coastal strip has been sacrificed to the expansion of the oil industry during the 20th century.

FAWLEY, THE CHURCH c1955 F150003

FAWLEY
The Church c1955
The church of All Saints at Fawley dates back to Saxon times, though much of the present building is Norman or later. The church was bombed in 1940, but has now been carefully restored.

FAWLEY
High Street c1955
Domesday Book describes Fawley as Falalie or Falegia and says that Walkelin, Bishop of Winchester, held as abbey lands 'one hyde and three yardlands'. The whole area was taken into the Forest by the Conqueror, though it was released for farmland in later centuries.

FAWLEY, HIGH STREET c1955 F150007

FAWLEY, THE FALCON INN c1955 F150008
Legend relates that it was close to here that the Saxon warlord Cerdic landed to begin the Saxon invasion of southern England, only to be thwarted by the British war-leader Arthur. The real-life Cerdic was probably the ancestor of the Saxon kings of Wessex.

FAWLEY, THE REFINERY c1965 F150020
In the 20th century, much of the low-lying marshlands around Fawley and Southampton Water beyond were given over to the import and refining of oil. Here we see a tanker unloading its cargo.

FAWLEY, ESSO OIL REFINERY c1955 F150001
The huge oil refinery at Fawley cost £120 million when it was built; it occupied the site of Cadland Park, the former home of the Drummond family. This refinery was the largest in the United Kingdom.

FAWLEY, ESSO HOUSE c1965 F150029
The 20th century's reliance on oil products provided for a profitable industry. This imposing suite of offices was built for the Esso Petroleum Company.

HIGHCLIFFE, THE CASTLE 1900 45059

Highcliffe Castle was once one of the grandest stately homes in England; a restoration programme is bringing it back to its former glory. The grade I listed building was built in the Romantic style by Lord Stuart de Rothesay between 1830 and 1835, employing the leading London architect William Donthorpe.

HIGHCLIFFE, LYMINGTON ROAD c1955 H295021

Highcliffe is the most easterly parish in Dorset, famous for its eroding cliffs and splendid views across to the Isle of Wight. This part of the coast makes a perfect touring centre for anyone wishing to explore both the New Forest and the Dorset countryside.

HYTHE, HIGH STREET c1955 H372001
In Victorian times Hythe was a mere village on the banks of Southampton Water, but it increased in size during the 20th century largely owing to the availability of employment at the nearby oil refinery at Fawley.

HYTHE, HIGH STREET c1955 H372009
Hythe was once the port of the New Forest; a settlement survived here after the Conquest, despite the excesses of William the Conqueror. The Forest now begins some distance away, though its heathlands still border the town.

HYTHE, ST JOHN'S STREET c1955 H372014
Hythe is now a popular residential area standing just across the water from the great city of Southampton. A ferry runs regularly to the latter from Hythe's pier, whilst not far away is Beaulieu Heath and the wild countryside of the New Forest.

HYTHE, FLYING BOATS c1955 H372015
Flying boats remained a common sight on Southampton Water during and after the Second World War. In that conflict they were mainly used for anti-submarine duties, though a minor passenger service utilising these aircraft existed in the peaceful days of the 1950s.

KEYHAVEN, THE WATERSIDE C1960 K146038
Sheltered from the sea by a spit of land called the Shingles is Keyhaven. Its marshes, tidal waters and mudflats are a favoured and sheltered spot for sailors and an important bird reserve.

LEPE, THE BEACH C1955 L482012
Lepe remains an attractive hamlet offering safe bathing in the waters of the Solent. In Roman times a road ran west from here across the present ground of the New Forest to Ringwood.

LEPE, THE BEACH c1955 L482014
Even half a century ago the relatively safe bathing at Lepe brought in thousands of tourists and the car parks were soon full on hot summer days. In the background is the Isle of Wight.

LYMINGTON, HIGH STREET 1952 L148045
Lymington, standing proudly above the short estuary of the Lymington or Boldre River, is first mentioned in the Domesday Book as Lentune, though a settlement existed here long before that. The old hillfort of Buckland Rings was certainly occupied by the Romans - nearly 2 hundredweight of Roman coins were found there in the 18th century.

LYMINGTON, THE FERRY c1955 L148016
Lymington serves as an important access port, offering one of the shortest passages across the Solent to Yarmouth and the Isle of Wight. Too many people rush through this fascinating old town in their hurry to reach the island over the water.

LYMINGTON, THE FERRY 'FARRINGFORD' c1955 L148120
Lymington has always been important as a port; it has not always been the small anchorage that visitors see today. During the Hundred Years War Lymington supplied far more ships for Edward III's invasion of France than neighbouring Portsmouth did.

LYMINGTON
High Street c1955

The Manor of Lymington was created at the time of the Conquest, and was granted to Earl Roger of Shrewsbury. Its importance probably lay in the salterns, or salt works, along the estuary and shoreline, which were first recorded in 1147.

◆

LYMINGTON
High Street c1955

Lymington's parish church at the western end of the High Street, with its prominent cupola and weather vane, was originally built in 1250, though it has many later restorations and additions.

LYMINGTON, HIGH STREET c1955 L148117

LYMINGTON, HIGH STREET c1955 L148022

LYMINGTON, QUAY HILL c1955 L148048
Lymington has connections with the famous. Edward Gibbon, the historian of the Roman Empire, was once its Member of Parliament. The Victorian poet Coventry Patmore lies buried in the churchyard, as is Caroline Bowles, the second wife of the Poet Laureate Robert Southey.

LYMINGTON, THE QUAY c1955 L148086
The presence of the Isle of Wight has given the waters around Lymington unusual double tides - a boon to yachtsmen in and around the little estuary.

LYMINGTON, VIEW FROM TOWN QUAY 1955 L148040
Lymington is surrounded by pleasant countryside, and the town makes an excellent base for exploring the New Forest. A footpath for ramblers leads around the coastline to Keyhaven, and the estuary provides a good introduction to the delights of boating.

LYMINGTON, THE HIGH STREET FROM THE CHURCH 1958 L148142
A splendid view down the High Street from the church tower in those halcyon days when there were fewer cars on the road - and when parking a motor vehicle presented few problems.

MILFORD ON SEA, HURST CASTLE c1955 M303166

Hurst Castle was built by Henry VIII between 1541 and 1544 as a defence against foreign attack, utilising many of the stones from the dismantled Beaulieu Abbey. King Charles I lodged here in 1648 on the way to his trial and execution.

MILFORD ON SEA, THE LIGHTHOUSE, HURST POINT c1955 M303145

At the end of the strip of land known as the Shingles is the lighthouse at Hurst Point, warning ships of the mudbanks and shallows that line the nearby coastline.

MILFORD ON SEA, HIGH STREET C1955 M303028
Milford on Sea has been a successful small resort since Victorian times, and its devotees return again and again. The beach is shingly, but the bathing is safe. There are a number of excellent country walks in the area, many of them boasting wonderful views across to the Isle of Wight.

MILFORD ON SEA, THE CHURCH C1955 M303094
Milford on Sea's present exquisite church started out in Norman times, though much of the surviving building is 13th-century. In the churchyard lies the eminent Victorian biologist William Saville Kent, who died in 1908, his grave covered with an array of fossilised sponges.

MILFORD ON SEA, HIGH STREET c1960 M303182

Milford on Sea's church, along with the one at Brockenhurst, was a survivor of the forest clearances and receives a mention in the Domesday Book. As a coastal village it survived the worst excesses of William the Conqueror's reign.

MILFORD ON SEA, THE GREEN c1955 M303027

The relatively low-lying ground around Milford on Sea makes the area ideal for exploration on foot or bicycle. Birdwatchers would do well to bring their binoculars the better to see the great variety of seabirds that visit this coastline.

Index

Frith Book Co Titles

Frith Book Company publish over a 100 new titles each year. For latest catalogue please contact Frith Book Co.

Town Books 96pp, 100 photos. County and Themed Books 128pp, 150 photos
(unless specified) All titles hardback laminated case and jacket
except those indicated pb (paperback)

Around Barnstaple	1-85937-084-5	£12.99
Around Blackpool	1-85937-049-7	£12.99
Around Bognor Regis	1-85937-055-1	£12.99
Around Bristol	1-85937-050-0	£12.99
Around Cambridge	1-85937-092-6	£12.99
Cheshire	1-85937-045-4	£14.99
Around Chester	1-85937-090-X	£12.99
Around Chesterfield	1-85937-071-3	£12.99
Around Chichester	1-85937-089-6	£12.99
Cornwall	1-85937-054-3	£14.99
Cotswolds	1-85937-099-3	£14.99
Around Derby	1-85937-046-2	£12.99
Devon	1-85937-052-7	£14.99
Dorset	1-85937-075-6	£14.99
Dorset Coast	1-85937-062-4	£14.99
Around Dublin	1-85937-058-6	£12.99
East Anglia	1-85937-059-4	£14.99
Around Eastbourne	1-85937-061-6	£12.99
English Castles	1-85937-078-0	£14.99
Around Falmouth	1-85937-066-7	£12.99
Hampshire	1-85937-064-0	£14.99
Isle of Man	1-85937-065-9	£14.99
Around Maidstone	1-85937-056-X	£12.99
North Yorkshire	1-85937-048-9	£14.99
Around Nottingham	1-85937-060-8	£12.99
Around Penzance	1-85937-069-1	£12.99
Around Reading	1-85937-087-X	£12.99
Around St Ives	1-85937-068-3	£12.99
Around Salisbury	1-85937-091-8	£12.99
Around Scarborough	1-85937-104-3	£12.99
Scottish Castles	1-85937-077-2	£14.99
Around Sevenoaks and Tonbridge	1-85937-057-8	£12.99

Sheffield and S Yorkshire	1-85937-070-5	£14.99
Shropshire	1-85937-083-7	£14.99
Staffordshire	1-85937-047-0 (96pp)	£12.99
Suffolk	1-85937-074-8	£14.99
Surrey	1-85937-081-0	£14.99
Around Torbay	1-85937-063-2	£12.99
Wiltshire	1-85937-053-5	£14.99
Around Bakewell	1-85937-113-2	£12.99
Around Bournemouth	1-85937-067-5	£12.99
Cambridgeshire	1-85937-086-1	£14.99
Essex	1-85937-082-9	£14.99
Around Great Yarmouth	1-85937-085-3	£12.99
Hertfordshire	1-85937-079-9	£14.99
Isle of Wight	1-85937-114-0	£14.99
Around Lincoln	1-85937-111-6	£12.99
Oxfordshire	1-85937-076-4	£14.99
Around Shrewsbury	1-85937-110-8	£12.99
South Devon Coast	1-85937-107-8	£14.99
Around Stratford upon Avon	1-85937-098-5	£12.99
West Midlands	1-85937-109-4	£14.99

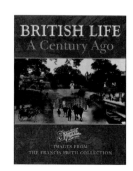

British Life A Century Ago
246 x 189mm
144pp, hardback.
Black and white
Lavishly illustrated with photos
from the turn of the century,
and with extensive commentary.
It offers a unique insight into
the social history and heritage
of bygone Britain.

1-85937-103-5 £17.99

Available from your local bookshop or from the publisher

Frith Book Co Titles Available in 2000

Around Bath	1-85937-097-7	£12.99	Mar
County Durham	1-85937-123-x	£14.99	Mar
Cumbria	1-85937-101-9	£14.99	Mar
Down the Thames	1-85937-121-3	£14.99	Mar
Around Exeter	1-85937-126-4	£12.99	Mar
Greater Manchester	1-85937-108-6	£14.99	Mar
Around Guildford	1-85937-117-5	£12.99	Mar
Around Harrogate	1-85937-112-4	£12.99	Mar
Around Leicester	1-85937-073-x	£12.99	Mar
Around Liverpool	1-85937-051-9	£12.99	Mar
Around Newark	1-85937-105-1	£12.99	Mar
Northumberland and Tyne & Wear			
	1-85937-072-1	£14.99	Mar
Around Oxford	1-85937-096-9	£12.99	Mar
Around Plymouth	1-85937-119-1	£12.99	Mar
Around Southport	1-85937-106-x	£12.99	Mar
Welsh Castles	1-85937-120-5	£14.99	Mar
Around Belfast	1-85937-094-2	£12.99	Apr
Canals and Waterways	1-85937-129-9	£17.99	Apr
Down the Severn	1-85937-118-3	£14.99	Apr
East Sussex	1-85937-130-2	£14.99	Apr
Exmoor	1-85937-132-9	£14.99	Apr
Gloucestershire	1-85937-102-7	£14.99	Apr
Around Horsham	1-85937-127-2	£12.99	Apr
Around Ipswich	1-85937-133-7	£12.99	Apr
Ireland (pb)	1-85937-181-7	£9.99	Apr
Kent Living Memories	1-85937-125-6	£14.99	Apr
London (pb)	1-85937-183-3	£9.99	Apr
New Forest	1-85937-128-0	£14.99	Apr
Scotland (pb)	1-85937-182-5	£9.99	Apr
Around Southampton	1-85937-088-8	£12.99	Apr
Stone Circles & Ancient Monuments			
	1-85937-143-4	£17.99	Apr
Sussex (pb)	1-85937-184-1	£9.99	Apr
Colchester (pb)	1-85937-188-4	£8.99	May
County Maps of Britain			
	1-85937-156-6 (192pp)	£19.99	May
Leicestershire (pb)	1-85937-185-x	£9.99	May

Lincolnshire	1-85937-135-3	£14.99	May
Around Newquay	1-85937-140-x	£12.99	May
Nottinghamshire (pb)	1-85937-187-6	£9.99	May
Redhill to Reigate	1-85937-137-x	£12.99	May
Victorian & Edwardian Yorkshire			
	1-85937-154-x	£14.99	May
Around Winchester	1-85937-139-6	£12.99	May
Yorkshire (pb)	1-85937-186-8	£9.99	May
Berkshire (pb)	1-85937-191-4	£9.99	Jun
Brighton (pb)	1-85937-192-2	£8.99	Jun
Dartmoor	1-85937-145-0	£14.99	Jun
East London	1-85937-080-2	£14.99	Jun
Glasgow (pb)	1-85937-190-6	£8.99	Jun
Kent (pb)	1-85937-189-2	£9.99	Jun
Victorian & Edwardian Kent			
	1-85937-149-3	£14.99	Jun
North Devon Coast	1-85937-146-9	£14.99	Jun
Peak District	1-85937-100-0	£14.99	Jun
Around Truro	1-85937-147-7	£12.99	Jun
Victorian & Edwardian Maritime Album			
	1-85937-144-2	£17.99	Jun
West Sussex	1-85937-148-5	£14.99	Jun
Churches of Berkshire	1-85937-170-1	£17.99	Jul
Churches of Dorset	1-85937-172-8	£17.99	Jul
Churches of Hampshire	1-85937-207-4	£17.99	Jul
Churches of Wiltshire	1-85937-171-x	£17.99	Jul
Derbyshire (pb)	1-85937-196-5	£9.99	Jul
Edinburgh (pb)	1-85937-193-0	£8.99	Jul
Herefordshire	1-85937-174-4	£14.99	Jul
Norwich (pb)	1-85937-194-9	£8.99	Jul
Ports and Harbours	1-85937-208-2	£17.99	Jul
Somerset and Avon	1-85937-153-1	£14.99	Jul
South Devon Living Memories			
	1-85937-168-x	£14.99	Jul
Warwickshire (pb)	1-85937-203-1	£9.99	Jul
Worcestershire	1-85937-152-3	£14.99	Jul
Yorkshire Living Memories			
	1-85937-166-3	£14.99	Jul

FRITH PRODUCTS & SERVICES

Francis Frith would doubtless be pleased to know that the pioneering publishing venture he started in 1860 still continues today. More than a hundred and thirty years later, The Francis Frith Collection continues in the same innovative tradition and is now one of the foremost publishers of vintage photographs in the world. Some of the current activities include:

Interior Decoration

Today Frith's photographs can be seen framed and as giant wall murals in thousands of pubs, restaurants, hotels, banks, retail stores and other public buildings throughout the country. In every case they enhance the unique local atmosphere of the places they depict and provide reminders of gentler days in an increasingly busy and frenetic world.

Product Promotions

Frith products have been used by many major companies to promote the sales of their own products or to reinforce their own history and heritage. Brands include Hovis bread, Courage beers, Scots Porage Oats, Colman's mustard, Cadbury's foods, Mellow Birds coffee, Dunhill pipe tobacco, Guinness, and Bulmer's Cider.

Genealogy and Family History

As the interest in family history and roots grows world-wide, more and more people are turning to Frith's photographs of Great Britain for images of the towns, villages and streets where their ancestors lived; and, of course, photographs of the churches and chapels where their ancestors were christened, married and buried are an essential part of every genealogy tree and family album.

A series of easy-to-use CD Roms is planned for publication, and an increasing number of Frith photographs will be able to be viewed on specialist genealogy sites. A growing range of Frith books will be available on CD.

The Internet

Already thousands of Frith photographs can be viewed and purchased on the internet. By the end of the year 2000 some 60,000 Frith photographs will be available on the internet. The number of sites is constantly expanding, each focussing on different products and services from the Collection.
Some of the sites are listed below.

www.townpages.co.uk
www.icollector.com
www.barclaysquare.co.uk
www.cornwall-online.co.uk

For background information on the Collection look at the three following sites:

www.francisfrith.com
www.francisfrith.co.uk
www.frithbook.co.uk

Frith Products

All Frith photographs are available Framed or just as Mounted Prints, and can be ordered from the address below. From time to time other products - Address Books, Calendars, Table Mats, etc - are available.

For further information:
if you would like further information on any of the above aspects of the Frith business please contact us at the address below:
The Francis Frith Collection,
Frith's Barn, Teffont, Salisbury, Wiltshire,
England SP3 5QP.
Tel: +44 (0)1722 716 376 Fax: +44 (0)1722 716 881   Email: uksales@francisfrith.com

---

To receive your FREE Mounted Print

Cut out this Voucher and return it with your remittance for £1.50 to cover postage and handling. Choose any photograph included in this book. Your SEPIA print will be A4 in size, and mounted in a cream mount with burgundy rule lines, overall size 14 x 11 inches.

Order additional Mounted Prints at HALF PRICE (only £7.49 each*)

If there are further pictures you would like to order, possibly as gifts for friends and family, acquire them at half price (no additional postage and handling required).

Have your Mounted Prints framed*

For an additional £14.95 per print you can have your chosen Mounted Print framed in an elegant polished wood and gilt moulding, overall size 16 x 13 inches (no additional postage and handling required).

---

* IMPORTANT!
These special prices are only available if ordered using the original voucher on this page (no copies permitted) and at the same time as your free Mounted Print, for delivery to the same address

---

Voucher for FREE and Reduced Price Frith Prints

Picture no.	Page number	Qty	Mounted @ £7.49	Framed + £14.95	Total Cost
		1	**Free of charge***	£	£
			£7.49	£	£
			£7.49	£	£
			£7.49	£	£
			£7.49	£	£
			£7.49	£	£
			* Post & handling		£1.50
Book Title			**Total Order Cost**		£

Please do not photocopy this voucher. Only the original is valid, so please cut it out and return it to us.

I enclose a cheque / postal order for £ . . . .
made payable to 'The Francis Frith Collection'
OR please debit my Mastercard / Visa / Switch / Amex card

Number . . . .

Expires . . . . Signature . . . .

Name Mr/Mrs/Ms . . . .

Address . . . .

. . . .

. . . .

. . . . Postcode . . . .

Daytime Tel No . . . .   Valid to 31/12/01

Frith Collectors' Guild

From time to time we publish a magazine of news and stories about Frith photographs and further special offers of Frith products. If you would like 12 months FREE membership, please return this form.

Send completed forms to:
The Francis Frith Collection, Frith's Barn, Teffont, Salisbury, Wiltshire SP3 5QP

The Francis Frith Collectors' Guild

Please enrol me as a member for 12 months free of charge.

Name Mr/Mrs/Ms . . . .

Address . . . .

. . . .

. . . .

. . . . Postcode . . . .

Free Print - see overleaf